A Life's Journey

Inspired By Life's Memories

Susan Linville Branin

ISBN 979-8-89043-660-3 (paperback)
ISBN 979-8-89043-661-0 (digital)

Copyright © 2024 by Susan Linville Branin

All rights reserved. No part of this publication may be reproduced, distributed, or transmitted in any form or by any means, including photocopying, recording, or other electronic or mechanical methods without the prior written permission of the publisher. For permission requests, solicit the publisher via the address below.

Christian Faith Publishing
832 Park Avenue
Meadville, PA 16335
www.christianfaithpublishing.com

Printed in the United States of America

Dedicated to everyone walking life's journey.

Preface

Parenting is not an easy thing to do. When your baby is born, you do not realize at that moment that your sweet, cuddly baby will grow up and go through a variety of changes, hormones, temperaments. You are just thinking about that precious baby that you have been blessed with and how honored you are to have such a wonderful new bundle of joy. This baby brings you so much happiness, and you find a love that is so different from any other love. I believe that when we see our children for the first time, our world changes, the way we think changes, and the way we love is different. Parenting brings to your attention and to your heart exactly what love truly is. The love you have for your child is a love that is so deep and strong, it is difficult to understand how one can love someone you just met so much.

I remember every second of the moment that I saw my first daughter for the first time after delivery. The nurse held her up for a brief second then immediately put an extremely small oxygen mask on her and rushed her to the nursery because she was not taking in oxygen as she should be. When the nurse held her up to me, I remember seeing that my baby girl had red hair. I will admit that I had said so many times that I want children, but I did not want any to have red hair, but the moment I saw her red hair and pink skin, I was awestruck. My heart was so happy and so full. After being taken to the nursery, I was not allowed to see her until her vitals and oxygen were normal. As I lay down in the hospital bed wondering how she was doing, wondering and wanting to hold my sweet baby, the door swung open, and I see my mother and my aunt and the nurse wheeling in the clear bassinet that babies are laid in after birth and my mother picking up my beautiful redheaded baby girl and handing her to me. At this moment, like many other new parents, my world completely changed. One year later, four days shy of my firstborn's first birthday, I gave birth to my second blessing. Another beautiful baby girl with sandy-blonde curly hair. She was perfect. The nurse immediately placed her on my chest, and I was once again in awe of this human being that God blessed and trusted me with.

Twenty-one years and three months later, my world changed yet again. My oldest daughter took her final breath and was taken from her temporary home on earth and taken to her permanent home in heaven. Losing my beautiful redheaded princess took me to a dark place. I was and still am lost. My heart has a void that I am not sure will ever be filled. There is a large piece of me that is missing, and it is so difficult to go from talking to her four or five times a day to not being able to talk to her at all. I miss her more than can be described. Later in this book, I will speak more on this and how this child is and will always be my hero.

If raising a child is not difficult enough, raising children with disorders makes the journey much more interesting and definitely a test of patience and understanding. Finding various methods of going through trials and difficulties are something that every parent will have to find for themselves. Advice can be given, of course, but that advice may not work the same for every child and every situation. At times, many times, you find yourself in more of a trial-and-error situation until you find the right path.

Please know that this book is not a book teaching you how to be a parent, but rather to let you know that you are not alone and to let you know that every moment is not blissful and definitely not easy, which makes all the wonderful and happy moments so special. It is my hope that this book will help you to be encouraged, uplifted, and given a sense of peace through the good times and bad. I, by no means, am a perfect mother, and there are things that I wish that I had done differently, and there are things that I am still learning. I am, however, a mother that loves her children unconditionally and would do anything for them and at one point begged and pleaded for my life to be taken rather than my daughter's life. God had different plans. Throughout this book, there will be personal experiences, failures, accomplishments, encouragements, and life-changing moments. Many of you might be able to relate, but I hope you all find peace and comfort in knowing that almost all parents go through similar situations. I also pray that my experiences, emotions, and trials and errors bring you some sort of comfort, understanding, and motivation to keep going and not give up. Times will be tough, but they will also be full of wonderful moments that you will cherish forever, and these moments will entirely outweigh the tough times. Let us walk together through this journey of life.

Chapter 1

Growing Up

Remember growing up and thinking that you could not wait to grow up and become an adult? I sure do, and now that I am an adult, I wonder what in the world was I thinking because adulthood is hard. We wanted to grow up so that we could make our own rules, stay out as late as we wanted, buy whatever we want, and no one could tell us no. I remember wanting to be a grown-up not because I disliked being a child, but I wanted to be able to do what I wanted to do whenever I wanted to. My childhood was a wonderful childhood. I had an amazing mother and father who worked so hard to make sure that my two brothers and I had everything that we needed—*needed* being the key word here. Our parents may have not been able to give us everything that we wanted, but we had food on the table, a roof over our heads, and we were greatly loved. As a child, one does not understand the phrase "we can't afford it" and did not like hearing the word *no* every time we asked for something. I just knew that when I grew up, I would buy whatever I wanted to buy, and I would make sure that my children had everything that they wanted. Fast-forward a few years, and did I buy everything that I or my children wanted? No. I had become my parents, which definitely was not a bad thing.

When I was around five or six years old, I remember that my best cousin had gotten a play kitchen for Christmas, and I was a bit jealous because I wanted a play kitchen. Every Christmas morning, she would call me and tell me what she had gotten and asked me what I had gotten, and this one year, I did not get what I had wanted. My parents just simply did not have the funds to buy something like that as our necessities were more important. Being a child, I did not understand this, but it was okay. I was able to play with her kitchen set when I would spend time with her. A couple of mornings after Christmas, my daddy did something for me that I will never forget.

 I had woken up and crawled out of bed, which was behind the sofa in the living room because we had a very small, very warm and cozy house, and I saw something in the opening between the living room and kitchen. I remember seeing my mother at the stove cooking breakfast, and my daddy was sitting on the sofa. I walked over to this large box in the opening, and I was so excited. My daddy had gotten a large square cardboard box, and he painted an oven door and knobs on the front and burners on the top. I could not wait to play with my new cardboard box oven. I had gotten some pots and pans from the cabinet and started pretend cooking and serving my daddy imaginary food. Even forty years later, that is still one of the fondest memories of my childhood and the best gift that I had ever received, and it cost nothing. I say this because our parents teach us lessons. They teach us that money and things do not make one happy; it is the moments in life that make us. They teach us how to live and how to thrive and survive. These are moments that we should cherish rather than rush through. How do you teach children this? Can you really teach children this lesson? I believe so, but it is not going to always be easy, but it can be done. For example, the best gifts cost nothing, and it comes directly from the heart. My very favorite gift that I have ever received as an adult is a letter that my daughter wrote to me. The words that she wrote down for me were extremely meaningful, and I could tell that it came straight from her loving heart. I still have the letter framed, and it sits on my dresser in my bedroom, and I read it often.

 Parenthood does not come with a manual. Parenting is something that you learn as you go, and your parenting style may not work the same for every child. If parenting isn't hard enough, now you have to have multiple styles of parenting depending on the child. Mom and Dad can use the exact techniques and use the same rules for all their children; however, each child is different, so one rule and technique that works for one child may not work for the other. They have their own temperaments—one may be dependent and the other independent, one may like to laugh and play all the time where the other wants to cry and throw temper tantrums. So now what? The differences in children are often blamed on the foods we eat such as preservatives, gluten allergies, dyes, etc., which may be true to an extent, but in reality, everyone is just different. I am not sure what your religion and beliefs are; however, I do believe in God, and I believe that God made us different from each other for a reason. If we were all the same, it could be a very boring world, don't you think?

I always knew that I wanted to be a mother one day, but I knew that I would need to learn how to be a mom. If you are like me, I like to watch people. I enjoy watching how they interact with others, watching their mannerisms and learning from them. I watched my grandparents interact with my aunts and uncles as adults, and I watched them interact with their grandchildren and great-grandchildren. My grandparents were excellent role models. They raised ten children, so they must have known what they were doing, right? I also had my own personal role models, my mother and father. They didn't know all the answers either, but they sure did a great job. Was everything always perfect? Of course not, but they were loving, caring, nurturing, provided for us, taught us the Bible and to love the Lord. There were moments where my brothers and I really tested our parents' tolerance, but they never gave up on us. There might have been some raised voices, some eye rolling, spanking, but we deserved it. They had every right to be angry or upset with us, but we always knew they loved us. It was because they loved us that they would be upset and concerned about things we did. They did not want us to fail. They did not want us to make not-so-smart decisions. They wanted to keep us safe, make wise choices and be honorable, honest adults. This is love.

Thinking back to when you were a child, what do you remember of your parents? Do you remember the good times, all the "I love yous," the hugs, etc., or do you remember and dwell on those times when there were disagreements, yelling, and door slamming? Why does it seem that we remember the not-so-good times more than the good times? Just like when one works hard and produces excellent work, no one acknowledges the good work, but when one makes one mistake, people make sure that that mistake is known. I never really thought about this happening until I became a parent. I want to share a personal experience of this. I remember when I was in sixth grade, in the library at school, I started my first monthly cycle. I was rather scared because I did not really know what it was, and my good friend explained to me what was going on. I was still scared about it and did not want to tell my mother. It didn't take long for my mother to find out, of course, and I remember sitting in my bedroom and my mother walking into my room holding a yellow plastic baseball bat. Before any conclusions are made, no, my mother was not an abusive mother. She was a very loving mother, and she was not coming in with the bat with the intention of using it. When I saw her walk in with this bat and saying, "We need to have a talk" as she sat down on the bench in front of my window, I remember my heart was beating so fast because I thought that I knew what she was going to talk about, but I didn't know if I had done something wrong and she was going to get onto me. Of course, she wasn't getting onto me. She was explaining what my body was doing and why. For years and years, I have told this story to others, and it wasn't until I became a mother that I realized that I needed to stop dwelling and telling this story. I wondered why this particular story always stood out to me, and I believe it was because of the yellow plastic bat. Why did she come in with this bat? I knew she wasn't going to do anything with it, but why did she have it? In all honesty, she was just as nervous as I was about having "the talk." The bat was a kind of a fidget spinner for her to ease her anxiety and nervousness. As an adult many years later, I asked her if she remembered this, and she did not; however, we do laugh about it now. I am sure that many of you can relate to something similar to this either as a child or as a parent.

As a teenager, I suffered with migraine headaches quite often. My mother would allow me to lay my head in her lap as she massaged my head to help ease the pain of the migraine. I also remember during church service every Sunday, my mother, if she was not in the choir, would lightly comb through my hair. I remember my daddy allowing me to lay my head on his shoulder and how one time my daddy tried to put my hair in a ponytail before school and didn't do that great of a job. Rather than getting upset that my ponytail was wrong, I should have been grateful to him for trying because that should have been a special moment. So why is it that we hang on more to what we think are bad times rather than the good times? I am not sure if there is really a clear-cut answer to this. Same with the yellow-bat moment. There was no reason for me to be scared. I should have been thanking and hugging my mother for taking the time to talk and explain everything to me.

Now I am grown up. I have been married, and I have had two beautiful daughters. I have always tried to be a good mom, but I am not perfect, no human being is, and I know that I have made mistakes. There have been times that I raised my voice to my daughters, I have had to put them in time-out or give them a spanking. Yes, I am a firm believer in spankings. I believe that if there were more spankings with children, our children would be a bit more respectful and take more responsibility for their actions, but that is another topic, and I do not want to offend anyone at all for believing something different. What I do hope is that my daughters always remember the good times, and when there were bad times, I hope that not only them but myself as well learned and grew from those times. I have noticed that one of my daughters used to, and occasionally still does, dwell upon negative moments that have happened in her life, whether it be me getting onto her, being bullied at school, her sister getting upset with her, or moments of a lack of self-esteem. At twenty years old, she is still learning not to dwell on those moments and to think more about all the good and fun times in her life. She is learning that her life is worth living and is learning that every day is a new day and no matter what transpires from day to day, she can and will overcome. This is something that most people are learning to do. Should we forget all negative events in our life? Let's see.

Chapter 2

Negativity into Positivity

Chapter 1 ended with the question, "Should we forget all negative events in our life?" My answer to this is no. To tell you just one thing about me is that I am a very optimistic person. I always try to find the good in everything and everyone. I have not always been this way, and it changed after I married the biological father of my children. Without going into much detail, it was a difficult marriage with a great deal of infidelity on his part and verbal and emotional abuse along with threats against my children. With the threats against my children, I thought that the only way that I could keep my daughter and my unborn daughter safe was to stay in a loveless, unfaithful marriage. Then one day it changed when my nine-month-old daughter was crying and he popped her in the mouth, telling her to stop crying. No, he did not pop her hard, and he did not do it in a mean fashion, but regardless, he did pop a nine-month-old for crying, and that was the final straw. I knew that I had to get my baby girl out of the negative, unhappy environment. I say all this to tell you how I turned two and half years of negativity and verbal and emotional abuse into being a positive person. It took a period of bad in order to change to good.

    Your life will never be happy and flawless all the time. There will be moments of happiness, sadness, anger, frustration, joy, and confusion. We typically are not prepared for all these moments as they sometimes change within just a few minutes. It would be nice if we are all happy all the time, but that is not logical. With all the emotions around us and frictions that try to stir up even more emotions, it is difficult to know how to be. Although we do not know when these emotions will change or how or why they will change, I believe that we can try to prepare ourselves, in a manner of speaking. It is my opinion that it all starts within ourself. I have witnessed that many times, a person may jump to a conclusion and react prematurely, which much of the time, results in an inaccurate assumption or overreaction, sometimes underreaction. So ask yourself these questions: How do you want to be? Do you want to only react at the surface, or do you want to look deep within and react with an emotion that will bring you some sort of joy and peace? I choose to find the peace in every situation. It doesn't always work out that way; however, I am going to give it my best shot because I do not want to live an unhappy life. In more recent times, which you will read about later, this has proven to be extremely difficult but not impossible.

    I have never and will never forget the negative moments in my life. Not any from my childhood, not any from my work experience, not any from my bad marriage, not any. What I have done and will continue to do is forgive those that hurt me and forgive myself for the mistakes that I have made then take that hurt and those mistakes and learn from them. I have learned what to look for in people. I have learned to avoid those who continuously drag me down and decided to find the positive in everything. This, at times, is not easy to do. I was angry at my ex-husband for years and years, and it kept me from being happy. How would that help me move on? It wouldn't. It just still allowed him to have control over me. I knew that I had to find it inside myself to forgive him for everything that he had done. I also had to forgive myself for errors that I made in our relationship and marriage. I knew that I could not blame him solely for everything. It took quite some time, but eventually I forgave him and myself. A weight was lifted off my shoulders, and my heart was a little less hardened, which freed up space for love and happiness. To forgive someone, you do not have to tell them you have forgiven them; forgiveness is in your heart. You are not forgiving them to make them feel better necessarily; you are forgiving them to release a stress or a burden within yourself. I have had friends that unknowingly hurt me, and I didn't think that I could stay mad at them for hurting me when they didn't even know. So again, I had to find it in my heart to forgive them and move on. I really should not say that "I had to" because I didn't have to—I wanted to. I didn't want that hurt hovering over me and interfering with my inner peace. Eventually, I became friends with one of them once again, and I will neither bring the issue up, nor will I hold the past over her head. I would rather focus on the current moments and any future moments. I am sure that there are people who I have somehow hurt that I do not know about that I hope they have forgiven me. I would like to know if I have hurt someone, and I would like to personally apologize for whatever it is that I had done. If there is anyone out there that I have, in some way or another, hurt or offended, I would like to personally apologize for hurting you.

There are some people that I have met in this world that actually enjoy living in the negativity. It is almost as if they thrive on sad stories and a great deal of drama. I am sure that you have known a person(s) like this. I do not have an answer for those people, but I believe it is just they have not found their way to look at things in a more positive manner. I am, by no means, saying that they are wrong in how they choose to live. I just believe that they would find more happiness and joy if they became just a little more optimistic and forgiving. Maybe even turn the other cheek and avoid things or people that are joy takers. It is going to be more difficult to be positive or even have good things happen for you if you are always surrounding yourself with doubters and downers. We live in a crazy world right now, a world full of crime, hatred, jealously, fear, confusion. You turn on the news and it is mostly bad and negative and political, which I think that we can all admit angers most people as it usually turns into a big debate. It is important to know what is going on in the world; however, it would be nice for the news to produce more stories of compassion, of hope, of rejoices, don't you think? Good stories are also a part of the world. One way that I removed negativity from my life is to stop watching and reading the news. Is there really a way to get the news medias to bring more lighthearted stories to their broadcasts? In these current days, I would hope that the people in the world would prefer seeing and hearing good news rather than all the bad. Several years ago, my oldest daughter was the focus on an ongoing story regarding epilepsy and her raising funds to receive a seizure response service dog. There was such a large response with this story, and there were so many people reaching out to us wanting to donate, wanting to pray with and for us, wanting more information regarding epilepsy. This is the type of news and articles that we need more of. When my precious daughter passed away in December 2022, I reached out to the media who previously did the stories on her, but this time, I wanted the story to be about the amazing, heroic firemen that did everything that they could to save her life. The editor responded to me and said that this was a heartwarming story, and she wanted some information from me so they could share our story. It has been just over a month, and I have yet to hear back from her, and I have sent follow-up emails. I am not upset at all by this, but this is the type of story that our world needs.

I chose to just live my life, continue to work and take care of my family and home. I chose to cherish every moment of life because life is way too short to stay focused on the bad things in life. There have been many people met that are true pessimists, and I have heard some say that being a pessimist is a bad trait, but I think that this trait could actually be good as they are prepared for anything. Being slightly pessimistic could save your life. This type of person would be prepared in the event of a disaster; they are always ready for something to happen. Being a realist is more of a "go with the flow" type of person. They are open to a variety of outcomes and are generally accepting of whatever the outcome may be and make any necessary adjustments that may be needed. Then there are optimists. These persons are typically looking at any and all positive outcomes and believe the good will trump evil doings. They look toward the future with confidence and positivity. Think about how you view the world. Are you a pessimist, optimist, or a realist? Personally, I find that I am more of an optimist with a touch of realist. I go into everything anticipating a good and positive outlook and am hopeful that the outcome will be the best outcome possible; however, the realist in me knows that not everything will have a happy ending, so I have to accept the outcome and go along with it. It may be good for us to have a combination of all three of these traits so that we are prepared to handle anything that comes our way.

Have you ever noticed how, for some reason, that bad things always seem to outdo the good things? I wonder why that is. On television, in the news, bad things seem to raise the ratings of a show or network. That could also happen with good things. I am sure that many of you have heard the saying "Smiles are contagious." As an optimist, I believe this to be true; however, over the past couple of years, the realist in me has proven this not to be so true, and I am having a difficult time accepting that. I give a smile or small grin to everyone I walk by and make eye contact whether I know them or not. I find that to be a friendly quality, a sense of security and confidence. Over the past couple of years though, I have seen less and less persons making eye contact and smiling at others in a friendly greeting. I blame this partly to society and technology. Society has become less physically social-oriented and more communication completely by text messaging or social media. If we would only put our phones down and enjoy the company that you are with.

Don't get me wrong, technology is a great thing, for the most part. With technology, medical treatments, and surgeries has improved by being less invasive, with quicker healing time. Technology has improved workload, bringing more efficiency by reducing the amount of time it takes to perform certain jobs and tasks. It allows for persons to have an e-commerce business to buy and sell online. Technology has been great for many things. Technology has also made us lazy. It has taken away personal social contact and communication, it has become babysitters to our children, and it really has consumed our lives.

Make memories. Cherish every moment you have with friends and family. So to answer the question on whether or not we should forget the negative events in our life, my answer is no, we should not forget. We should take those moments and change the way we think about those moments. Take them and learn from them. Learn how to turn the negative into positives. Believe me, it will make you a happier or more prosperous person. It is time to get back to the basics and put the phones or other electronics down and focus on the people around you. Be the change.

Chapter 3

The Basics

The "basics" in life could and most likely will vary from person to person. Different cultures may have a different meaning of the basics; however, there are a few that I believe are universal. We have come to be too dependent on electronics, which in turn diverts us from the simpler things in life. Simplistic is quite often a better way to live life. Our lives have become so busy and hectic that we find shortcuts to get through the day. There are times that we may have to use shortcuts, but when we have those moments to just sit back, relax and put the electronic devices down for a bit, you may soon notice a change in your mindset.

When I was growing up, there were no cell phones, no texting, no Facebook, no Twitter, or Instagram. Our social media was being with our friends and talking verbally to one another and interacting. There were time limits on television time. After school, you come home, do homework, eat supper, then maybe watch some television with your family. We always ate as a family. Although we did not eat in a dining room, we ate together in the living room. On the weekends, we played outside, and if we came inside, we had to help clean house, so we always found things to do outside. We actually played in the dirt, played hide-n-seek, chase, tag, even used lawn and leaf trash bags to make our own Slip 'N Slide to play in the water. We had a great time and made such wonderful memories. In middle school, the infamous pagers/beepers came out. You were cool if you had a beeper. If someone needed to talk to you, they would page you, and you would have to find a pay phone to call that person back. Those were good times, simple times. Nowadays, it is not often that you go to a restaurant and see the patrons visiting with the person sitting across or next to them. Instead, most times, everyone at the table is on their phone on social media or talking to people that they are not currently with. What is the point of going to eat with someone if you are not going to visit with them? Some would think that it is mostly the younger generations that do this; that is not the case. Many of the older generations are on their phones. Then I see parents put iPads or tablets or phones in front of their toddlers at the restaurant to keep them entertained. I understand why the parents are doing this, but maybe just take the time to interact with the child and teach them how to behave while in public. We are teaching our children to rely solely on electronics to entertain and keep them quiet.

    I am by no means judging anyone or telling anyone how to behave or raise their children. I am just wanting to point out how we can get back to the basics. This next point is going to be a little hypocritical of everything said in the above paragraph as a Facebook post just popped up on my notifications, and I did stop writing to look at it because of the subject matter in the preview of the notification, and lo and behold, it goes with the point I am trying to make. You may have never heard of the *Andy Griffith Show* and if not, I encourage you to stream it and watch it. Not only is it quite comical, but there are also so many valuable lessons to be learned. The *Andy Griffith Show* is a television show from the 1960s about a widowed sheriff living with his son (Opie) and Aunt Bea, and he had a deputy, Barney, who liked to give Andy a challenge. Andy taught his son life lessons and wanted him to learn the basics of life. I am quoting from a Facebook post from Fox Sports Radio 1400 Texarkana, which is, "When Barney told Andy he should just let Opie decide for himself how he wanted to live, Andy had these words of wisdom. No, I'm afraid it don't work that way. You can't let a young's decide for himself. He'll grab at the first flashy thing with shiny ribbons on it. Then when he finds out there's a hook in it, it's too late. Wrong ideas come packaged with so much glitter that it's hard to convince 'em that other things might be better in the long run. All a parent can do is say 'wait' and 'trust me' and try to keep temptation away." This is so true. It is time again for parents to be parents and teach their children rather than being their child's friend or using television, phones, or tablets to entertain them. Play with them, teach them how to play tag or make mud pies, without the use of technology. Teach them right from wrong, teach them honesty, teach them to be sensitive toward others, teach them how to be social, how to work, how to be respectful, how to love, how to be humble, how to be a good person. Be an interactive parent, not a parent that is so busy that they lose precious time that cannot be gotten back. When my children were very young, I did allow them to watch shows as *Blue's Clues, Dora the Explorer, Barney, Veggie Tales* and others, but there were limits on how long I would allow them to watch. I did not want their imagination and vision to be distorted by things they saw on the television. Once they became of school age, there was a rule that homework and chores had to be completed before they were allowed to watch television or play games. This not only teaches responsibility, but also teaches them that at times, they can be rewarded for working hard and taking care of what needs to be taken care of. This is all part of the basics of life.

So what exactly would you say are the basics of life? The basics may mean something different to everyone, but the basics are rather simple, literally. In order to survive, we need food, water, shelter, clothing, and health. We do not need designer clothing, we do not need electronic devices, we do not need social media, we do not need high-speed internet or Wi-Fi. There was a time when I was looking at new refrigerators because I felt that my current one was about to go out on me. I was blown away at selection of refrigerators that are made now. There are some that talk to you, some that will keep a grocery list for you of the items you are out of, some that have multiple drawers for storage. I would prefer just a plain and simple *basic* refrigerator that keeps my food and drinks cold and my meats frozen. I do not care to have all that added fancy additions to a refrigerator. It is just silly to spend thousands of dollars on a refrigerator that talks to you or keeps a list for you. Just grab a pen and paper and write a list of your needs. This brings me to smart devices for your home that will turn on your lights, change your thermostat, operate your television, even operate your microwave oven. Is that really necessary? What blows my mind more than anything regarding these smart devices is that you can use it to control your microwave. Does the device put your food in the microwave for you? Of course not, you have to actually put the food in yourself, so why do you need a computer to put the cook time in? Can't you just push the button or two and hit Start since you are standing there putting your food in? To me, this is just laziness. Now I can understand if someone has a disability and these smart devices actually are beneficial to them, but overall, we are just becoming lazy creatures.

I am reminded of the movie *WALL-E*. Everyone on the ship was severely obese because all they did was sit in a moving chair and drink their meals and watch whatever was on the screen in front of them. At the end of the movie, they realized that they could actually get out of the chair and physically walk and saw that there was so much around them that they were missing or did not know existed. It seems like this is where we are headed in the world, just sitting around, gaining large amounts of weight, and being glued to a television screen. That is a scary thought. There is a world outside with much to do and much to take in and enjoy. I like watching a little television and playing a video game from time to time, but I love going outside for fresh air. I love spending time with family and friends. I love visiting and laughing with everyone, and it is so good for the soul.

Proverbs 15:16–26 in the Bible, New King James, says,

> Better is a little with the fear of the Lord, than great treasure with trouble. Better is a dinner of herbs where love is, than a fatted calf with hatred. A wrathful man stirs up strife, but he who is slow to anger allays contention. The way of the lazy man is like a hedge of thorns, but the way of the upright is a highway, A wise son makes a father glad, but a foolish man despises his mother. Folly

> is joy to him who is destitute of discernment, but a man of understanding walks up rightly. Without counsel, plans go awry, but in the multitude of counselors they are established. A man has joy by the answer of his mouth, and a word spoken in due season, how good it is! The way of life winds upward for the wise, that he may turn away from hell below. The Lord will destroy the house of the proud, but He will establish the boundary of the widow. The thoughts of the wicked are an abomination to the Lord, but the words of the pure are pleasant.

Ephesians 5:15–16 says, "Be very careful, then, how you live, not as unwise but as wise, making the most of every opportunity, because the days are evil."

I am sure that most of you would agree that our days are numbered and the world has become more evil, so wise choices should be made, and we should make the most out of each and every day. We do not have time to waste solely on the conveniences of technology, and we need to spend more time with family, being productive and optimistic on life.

> Do not conform to the pattern of this world, but be transformed by the renewing of your mind. Then you will be able to test and approve what God's will is, His good, pleasing, and perfect will. (Romans 12:2)

Chapter 4

Dating, Then Comes Marriage

Now that you have read about the basics and growing up with those basics, you enter into a new stage in life: dating! You are young, enjoying life, spending time with your friends and family, dating and trying to find the person that you want to spend the rest of your life with, the person that makes you whole. When finding that person, make sure that you both are equally yoked, have similar beliefs. The New King James version of the Bible in 2 Corinthians 6:14–18 states,

> Do not be yoked together with unbelievers. For what do righteousness and wickedness have in common? Or what fellowship can light have with darkness. What harmony is there between Christ and Belial? Or what does a believer have in common with an unbeliever? What agreement is there between the temple of God and idols? For we are the temple of the living God. As God has said, I will live with them and walk among them, and I will be their God, and they will be my people. Therefore, come out from them and be separate, says the Lord. Touch no unclean thing, and I will receive you, and I will be a Father to you, and you will be my sons and daughters, says the Lord Almighty.

What does it mean to be "equally yoked"? To be equally yoked means that you are in agreement with each other on most things, especially in your beliefs. You work together. You have the same goal, similar beliefs. Does this mean that you should not socialize with someone who is unequally yoked from you? I am no theologian and am by no means a perfect or even mediocre Christian, but it is my own opinion that the answer to that is no. If we never socialize with someone that is not our equal, we might lose a chance to lead someone to Christ. I believe that we need to be strong enough in our faith in Christ to be with others that are not as strong in their faith in Christ. Hopefully, you can be a witness to those and be a light to shine brightly in the love of Christ and lead others to also become a light in Christ.

In 1998, I met a man, and he and I began dating. I met him in a nightclub, and he worked the front door in checking IDs to make sure those coming in were of age. He and I immediately hit it off, and once his shift was over, we went out and spent some time getting to know one another. We started dating soon after that. There were many ups and downs in our relationship, but I thought that I truly loved him. Actually I didn't think I was. I *knew* that I was in love with him. He made the decision to go back to school in the Dallas area and asked me to move to the Dallas/Irving area. Without hesitation, I decided to move with him. I knew that he did not have any type of relationship with the Lord and I did, and there were doubts within our relationship, but I moved with him anyway in hopes that I could win him over to the Lord. Once we moved to Irving, our relationship began to change. Without going into a long, drawn-out story, because that could be a book in itself, there began a great deal of infidelity on his part, and I would come home from work to find different women in our apartment, and of course, there was always an explanation of why they were there.

I was a very naive person at that time in my life, and I let "love" overpower me, and I forgave a little too quickly. There was one day that I was working a double shift with a couple hour break in between shifts. Since we did not live far from my job, I drove home to take a quick nap. I was woken up by my now fiancé tickling my feet. I was confused on why he was home because he was supposed to be in class and was really confused when I turned my head and found a woman standing there with the brightest pink hair that I had ever seen. I asked who this was, and he said she was a beautician and he had a class with her and she was in need of a place to stay for a bit. I get up out of the recliner and noticed several suitcases and personal belongings of this woman. Again being naive, I agreed to let her stay with us until she got back on her feet. That evening, we went to bed, and this woman was asleep on our sofa in the living room. I woke up the next morning and realized my fiancé was not in our bed, so I got up to see where he was at. I walked around the bed and tripped over something. I turned the light on and saw that he and her were asleep together on the floor at the end of our bed. I will not go into detail what happened; however, I made sure she was out of the apartment soon after that.

After many apologies and promises from him that it would never happen again, I forgave him, and we moved on. Our relationship was never easy, and I caught him many times having affairs. By this time, all I wanted to do was leave, but he had spent all the money we had in our checking account. I approached my neighbors who were aware of the situation, and they pitched in for gas money so that I could get out there and go back home to my parents and get out of this damaging relationship. After being back home with my parents for a couple of weeks, I learned that I was five weeks pregnant. At first, I was shocked of this because I had been informed by a doctor that the chances of me becoming pregnant were slim to none because of particular medical issues I had when I was eighteen to nineteen years of age. Quickly, I became excited but scared to have to tell him. He already had four other children by two different women, and I knew how he was with them but hoped he would be better with our child. I told him the news over the phone then drove to Dallas to talk to him about it in person.

After several weeks, we were talking again, and things were going great. We were both excited to be having a baby together, and he asked me if we could put the past behind us then asked me to marry him. Without hesitation, I quickly said yes. If you are like my mother, you are shaking your head and asking the question, "Are you stupid? He has not changed, and you and that baby are going to be hurt!" I was love-stricken though and had a beautiful human being growing inside of me. In order to rid him of his temptations, we agreed to move out of the Dallas/Irving area and moved to a smaller town a little closer to home where our families were. I was all for moving and getting away from the past and creating a better future. Two weeks before our daughter was born, we had a very small wedding ceremony, and everything was back on track.

It is now September 2001, and the day before 9/11, I gave birth to our beautiful redheaded baby girl. He never left my side, and I was on cloud nine. The morning after she was born, he turned the television on in my hospital room, and all over every channel was the plane crashing into the twin towers in New York. It was an awful moment in our country's history, and all I wanted was the nurse to bring our baby in from the nursery. We were able to go home the next day, and once we did, our relationship started to go downhill again. To make a long story very short, there was a great deal of emotional, verbal, and physical abuse going on that I had to get out of this relationship and take our baby girl out of the evil that was taking place in our house. He had blown the engine on my car, so I could not just load up and leave. There were threats made that if I was to leave, I would never see my daughter again, so I thought the only way of protecting her was to stay in this nightmare. During the days, he would constantly keep a watch on me and would leave work at random times to make sure I was still at the house, so I wasn't sure how I was going to pull off leaving. One night after him popping our nine-month-old baby for crying, I knew that I had to get her out of there. I was not allowed to have a phone, so I had to save and hide quarters and find a pay phone to call my parents at just the right moment to come pick up myself and my baby girl. Since I had no vehicle, I had to put her in a stroller and walk to wherever I could to find a pay phone, which are not easy to find anymore. Finally, the day came that I knew I would be able to get out without him knowing, so my daughter and I walked across the street to a school's administration office and begged them to allow me to make a long-distance phone call. Seeing that something was wrong, they allowed me to make this call to my parents telling them to come get us and we only had about a two-hour window. Needless to say, my parents showed up in the nick of time and got us out of there. I did not even have time to get much. I just made sure to pack some diapers, formulas, bottles, and just threw a few clothes in a bag and left the house as soon as my parents showed up.

This is just a rather quick version of my story on marriage, and clearly we were not equally yoked, and anytime that I asked him to go to church with myself and our daughter, he refused. I believe he did go with me one time, but that was it. If we had the same beliefs and chose to live by God's word, I do think that we would have had a better marriage and a marriage that lasted with honesty, faithfulness, and love. After filing for divorce, I realized that I was twenty weeks pregnant with our second child, and I did let him know but refused to go back to him and chose to raise these babies as a single mother. This, I thought, would be a hard decision to make, but I would do it again in a heartbeat to make sure that my children were not raised in an evil environment and they would always know how much they are loved and would show them what love truly is. My daughters deserved to live in a happy home even if they only had one parent, but in their case, they had a loving mother and wonderful grandparents that allowed us to live with them until I was able to get a job so that I could find another place to live.

By telling a very summarized version of my marriage experience above, I hope that it is an encouragement to others to find a mate that is equally yoked because I guarantee it will help your marriage. I cannot guarantee that you will have a perfect marriage because I do not believe that exists, but I am most confident that with God as a foundation in your relationship, your marriage will be much better. Christ should be the center of all relationships. I hear often that a marriage is between two persons; in reality, it is between three, the two of you and God. Let Him be the foundation of the marriage and the household. It will not always be easy, and there will be difficult times, but with the Lord as your foundation, it will be stronger.

Chapter 5

Bringing Home Baby

The day comes that you find out a baby is on the way. How do you feel about that? Babies truly are a blessing. They are a gift loaned to us by our heavenly Father. We should cherish this time and the baby to come. God chose you to be the parent and to raise a child. As you wait these nine months for this baby to arrive, many thoughts run through your mind. These thoughts vary from happiness to fear then back to happiness. It is really a repetitive cycle. You wonder if you are going to know what to do when the baby comes. You wonder if the baby is going to be healthy. Then you stop and think that this baby coming is a blessing like no other. As a woman, I can't speak for the father-to-be, but something changes when you find out you are going to be a mother. You already possess wisdom, but the moment you find out you are going to be a mother, the amount of wisdom and knowledge increases. You learn what love truly is and how much love that you can store in your heart.

When I first learned I was pregnant with my first daughter, my entire outlook on life immediately changed. I was not married, and I had recently broken up with the father of my child. All I could think about was keeping my daughter safe and protecting her in every way that I could. This did not start after she was born; this started the moment I learned that I was having a baby. In addition to thinking about keeping my daughter safe and protected, I thought about being able to take care of this baby financially. How will I afford formula, diapers, clothes, doctor visits, etc. It is amazing at all the thoughts that a mother has when she is expecting. Our mind is constantly turning and constantly worrying and loving this baby even before this precious gift is born. It is okay to worry, it is normal to worry and I believe that it is good to worry. That means that you have your baby's best interest at heart, and you will do anything and everything that you can to raise this child in the best way you know how, and you will keep this wonderful baby safe.

Midway through the pregnancy, I had a sonogram of the baby and purchased a frame to put the sonogram picture in, and on the outside of the frame, my mother wrote this psalm on it:

> For you created my inmost being; you knit me together in my mother's womb. I praise you because I am fearfully and wonderfully made. (Psalm 139:13–14)

I fell in love with these words, so I continued to read the remainder of that passage, 15–18, which states,

> Your works are wonderful, I know that full well. My frame was not hidden from you when I was made in the secret place, when I was woven together in the depths of the earth. Your eyes saw my unformed body; all the days ordained for me were written in your book before one of them came to be. How precious to me are your thoughts, God! How vast is the sum of them! Were I to count them, they would outnumber the grains of sand when I awake, I am still with you.

These words spoke volumes to me as I knew that God was giving me the greatest gift and that was being a mother to one of His children. I will admit that I was very nervous about having a baby, not just the delivery, but the raising of a child, a child that I am being honored with. Will I have what it takes to raise a daughter that is honest, that is strong, that is moral and God fearing. This passage did help in easing some of this fear, and I know that I have to do my absolute very best in raising this child that belongs to God.

Nine months of preparation, nine months of feeling and watching this baby form and grow inside your womb. You have gotten the car seat, you have the crib and what you think are enough diapers. You have everything ready for your baby to be here. You have waited, you have wept, you have feared, you have prepared, you have prayed, and then the day finally comes. It is delivery day. It is so difficult, almost impossible to describe the emotions and the pain that will be endured over the next several hours while the mom-to-be is in labor. The contractions come and become a little more intense as time passes. Honestly, while in labor, having the very uncomfortable contractions, time seems to stand still. You focus on breathing, then during some moments, you forget how to breathe. You might even speak some not-so-kind words to whomever might be in the room with you and may not even care if you hurt their feelings. They will just need to understand and know that you do not mean those hurtful words at that moment. Your world and theirs is about to change, and the months of pregnancy and hours of labor are about to completely worth it.

Finally, the doctor says that it is time to push, and you are so exhausted and do not think that you can push anymore, but you do because you know that you have to. Moments later, you hear the most beautiful cry of a brand-new life that God has blessed you with and has entrusted you to raise.

> The word of the Lord came to me, saying, Before I formed you in the womb, I knew you; before you were born, I set you apart; I appointed you as a prophet to the nations. (Jeremiah 1:4–5)

Although the Lord was speaking to Jeremiah, I believe that He is speaking to all His people. He knew each of us before we were formed, and we are to speak out in His name, speak of His name, share His name, His love, His death to save us. He created us. He knew us before we were created. He sacrificed His son for each of us. Shouldn't we raise this beautiful child of His in His image? What does "His image" really mean? In my opinion, I take this to mean that we are to raise our children with morals that are pleasing to Him. We are to teach them to pray, teach them to spread His word. We are to make sure that our children are respectful to others, teach them to help those in need, to be true to themselves, sing His praises. We are all going to fail. Our children are going to have moments in which they fail by making a bad decision, but how we come back from that failure matters. We have to admit our failures and our wrongdoings, learn from them, and do better the next time. Seek the Lord's forgiveness. Seek your own forgiveness and move forward.

It is now time to bring your baby home from the hospital. What now? These two words will have one of the greatest impacts on me later in life, which I will speak of later. I ask you to store the two words, *what now*, in the back of your mind for now. You have the baby home. You are so tired. Your home is filled with visitors that want to hold and love on this new bundle of joy, but we keep going, and we keep our eyes wide open because we have this new responsibility to care for. In the beginning, you have a great deal of help to care for baby and to let you get some rest, but soon everyone will be going home, and it is just you and baby. You learn what sleepless nights are like. You learn how to change diapers and feed the baby in the middle of the night all with no sleep yourself. There were times when I felt as if I needed to get some strong duct tape to tape my eyelids open. In all reality, you start to forget how tired you are after a while. I believe that God made women special so that they could handle the lack of sleep and the strength to keep going. He made us women to be able to handle a great deal of pain and the ability to multitask in a way that you never thought possible. I am not intentionally leaving the men out because there are some amazing daddies out there that are great with their baby.

Did you ever think that you would know how to dress, cook, clean, etc. with one hand while the other hand is holding a baby? I, like many parents, learned to drive with their left hand while reaching back holding a bottle in the baby's mouth to feed. I gave birth to my second daughter only four days before my oldest daughter's first birthday. This gives an entire new meaning to the word *multitasking*. I now had two babies, one on each hip, still trying to shop for necessities, cook, clean, work. I was a single mother, and I was extremely grateful that I had my parents that helped me a great deal. Knowing how difficult it was to raise two babies only twelve months apart, I can't imagine what it is like for parents that have multiple births. I can relate to those parents of twins, but triplets or more is not even imaginable to me.

Being a new mom definitely was not always easy, but it was incredibly rewarding. I was infatuated with my daughters. I loved watching them grow. I love watching them play. When they would learn something new, I would make a big deal about it, and of course, they didn't understand why I was making a big deal when they rolled over for the first time and when they used the potty for the first time. They would get so excited playing peekaboo, and we acted as if we were really hiding and that they couldn't see us when we were hiding our eyes. Both of my girls loved when I would play patty-cake with them and always laughed. This brought me so much joy. My oldest daughter, Micayla, loved being the center of attention, and she would sing and dance, and when I had the video camera out, she made sure that she was the focus of attention. My youngest daughter, Savannah, was never one for the camera, and she always tried to get her sister to play with her.

This mom thing was becoming not as difficult as I thought it would. I do not know what I had to worry about when I was pregnant. We were having fun. They loved to play. They loved watching *Blue's Clues* and *Veggie Tales*. (If you haven't watched *Veggie Tales*, I encourage you to watch these short shows and movies.) They were learning new things every single day, and they sure knew how to brighten my days. My sassy redheaded britches and my curly-haired jokester each had completely different temperaments and personalities, but they were so precious, fun, and rewarding. Now don't get me wrong, they fought. They were both stubborn in their own way, but they sure missed each other when the other wasn't there or when the other was taking a nap. These two baby girls have become my everything, the absolute light of my life. As these two girls of mine grew, time seemed to go faster and faster, and I just wished that life would slow down.

When my second born was only two weeks old, I had to go back to work. We were currently living with my parents, who at that time were going through some difficult times. I am grateful that allowed my daughters and I to live with them until I was back on my feet again after separating from my husband. My mom and daddy were such a help with the girls, and there were nights that my youngest just did not want to sleep at all and I was so exhausted, so my mom would wake up and come in the living room and take over rocking her so that I could rest. Just as I would fall asleep, my oldest would wake up. I felt like a yo-yo many times because when I would get one baby to sleep, the other would wake up. It was back-and-forth all night. I don't believe I got my first full night's sleep since becoming a mom until twenty years later, and even now, there are nights that I do not sleep through the night, but that is because of heartache, which will be brought to light in an upcoming portion of this book.

I remember one night, I had gotten both girls to sleep and tucked into their beds. My oldest, Micayla, slept in a small toddler bed, and my youngest, Savannah, was in a crib as she was just a couple of months old. I got up out of my bed during the night to check on them and saw that Savannah was still asleep, but Micayla was not in her bed. I went into panic mode and searched all over the house for her and could not find her. I, now panicking, went into my parents' bedroom and woke them up to help me find her. We are frantically looking everywhere, and I went back into my parents' room, knelt down on my knees, and I see a small amount of her beautiful red hair sticking out from under their bed. My heart melting and with tears rolling down my face, I wrapped my arm around her belly and pulled her out from under the bed and just held her, then carried her and laid her in my bed, where I held her the rest of the night. I had caught her several times sleepwalking and would gently put her back in her bed. To this day, I still do not know why she would sleepwalk, and there were times that I would be scared to go into a deep sleep because I wanted to be able to hear her if and when she would crawl out of bed.

    Then we have my sweet Savannah. She was a very curious, free-spirited, hilarious, temperamental child. She always kept us all on our toes. One second she would be right beside you and the next second she had run off. We definitely had to keep our running shoes on with her. On an afternoon, the girls and I were outside with my parents, and I needed to run down the gas station and would only be gone for about ten minutes, so my mom said that they would watch the girls until I got back. When I pulled back in the driveway, I see my mother on the porch with Micayla and Savannah, and she appeared to be a little distraught. I asked her if everything was okay, and she told me that Savannah slipped away from their eyesight for a brief moment, and after hearing a car horn, they quickly turned to find Savannah had walked out into the road. She was so quick to slip away because her curiosity and free spirit was so high, she did what she wanted to do despite repercussions. Another time, as both girls were asleep, I decided to take that time to take a quick shower. While in the shower, I heard what sounded like the front door opening. Knowing that my parents were not home, I jumped out of the shower real fast, wrapped a towel around me, ran to the front door, and saw Savannah once again walking toward the road. I ran out in my towel, grabbed her, and ran back inside. Since she had figured out how to unlock and open the front door, that evening a lock was put on the top of the front door out of her reach so that she could no longer sneak out.

    Now that they are both toddlers, it was really time to get my running shoes on. They both kept everyone on their toes, and I would run after them over and over again. They were so much fun. These two sisters had such different personalities. My oldest wanted everyone's attention, and she would do this by singing and dancing or just coming up and sitting in your lap. My youngest, on the other hand, just wanted the attention from her sister. She adored her sister and just wanted more than anything for her sister to play with her. Big sister was quite bossy and wanted it her way, and the youngest would get her feelings hurt and then would throw a fit about it. She was the best at fit throwing. When they would actually play together, they played well, and I greatly enjoyed watching them spend good quality time together and learn from one another.

Chapter 6

Changes

When my baby girls were three and four years old, it was time to start looking for a place to live outside of my parents' house. At this time in my life, I was employed at a financial institution and had become friends with one of my coworkers. She and I became best friends, and she was like a sister that I never had the opportunity of having. I was blessed with two older brothers but always wanted a sister to bond with. Now, at first, I will admit that I was actually a little scared of her because she wasn't the easiest to talk to, but once I got to know her, she instantly became family and the absolute best friend ever. She spent time helping me to find a rent house, but unfortunately I was not yet able to afford a place of my own just yet. Being who she is, she offered to let my daughters and I stay at her house until I had enough saved up to obtain my own place. Seventeen years later, I am still here. My oldest daughter instantly took to my best friend, but my youngest took quite a bit longer. She was never one for change and was shy around new people.

When you find a great friend that will be there for you through thick and thin, you hold on and cherish that friendship. She gave my children and me a place to live when I was unable to find anything else in my price range. With her help and support, I was able to raise my children, give them everything that they needed. I was able to go back to school and earn my degree. Through the death of both of my grandparents, my father, and recently, my oldest daughter, she has never left my side. This is why I consider her my sister and not just a best friend. People like her are few and far between, and I am proud to call her my sister, my best friend. Her mother and father should be very proud of the daughter they raised. I do not know where I would be without her support and friendship. It has now been seventeen years since my daughters and I first moved in with her, and yes, I am still here because it is difficult to leave your support system, and I do not know where I would be today if it were not for her. I encourage you all to find that support. Find that person that will encourage you and lift you up without any judgment or ridicule.

After moving in, in preparing the kids' bedroom, I had bought them a set a bunk beds, and my youngest just had to have the top, which was fine with me. She had no trouble climbing the ladder to get to the top bunk, but getting down was always a struggle and a crying fest with her. The first couple of times, she did fine getting down the ladder, but that evening, she mysteriously had forgotten how to put her leg over the railing to put her foot on the ladder. I was in there with her trying to help her, and she would cross her little arms and scrunch up her sweet little face and whine, "I can't do it." Over and over, she just could not figure out how to climb down the ladder. I am doing my best to keep from laughing at her cute scrunched, frustrated face and trying to help her put her leg over the railing. After about fifteen minutes, she finally decided that she could do it. I have all this on a video camera, and watching back on it now just makes me giggle a lot. She was a very stubborn young lady, but she was also very sensitive and loved to help out. This child was adventurous and loved trying new things and really loved playing outside collecting grasshoppers.

The oldest was just happy wherever the adults were because she was a big "nosey-rosy." She always felt as if she was going to miss out on something so she wanted to stay around the people to know everything that was going on. Secrets definitely could not be kept around her. She was always good at telling others what their Christmas gifts were or just spilling the beans at whatever she could. Both of these girls loved one another so much. Like many siblings, they fought a lot, but they missed each other so much when they were apart. I always wanted them to be best friends and have a wonderful relationship with one another. I worried that since they did argue and disagree with each other, that the friendship never would build into anything. They both received much encouragement, but they still butted heads; however, I still knew that one day they would build a great relationship together.

Now a year has passed since moving, everyone is adjusting well. Both girls are now in school, one in kindergarten and one in pre-K. Savannah enjoyed staying in her room reading or playing games, Micayla still enjoyed being in the living room with the adults. Things are going great, then suddenly, our lives changed. Micayla had had allergy troubles since she was first born. She could not take breast milk, and she could not drink baby formula of any kind. The pediatrician finally instructed me to give her Silk soy milk, and that was the only thing she could drink as a newborn without completely hurting her tummy. She was allergic to so many things such as eggs, peanut butter, melons of all kinds, Cheetos, which all sent us to the emergency room so many times. After working with a dietician for a while, she was finally able to eat everything she had been allergic to or sensitive to except for melons, which still caused allergic reactions when she became an adult. These allergies soon became the least of our worries with her.

One evening, I was sitting on the sofa watching a little television. The girls were in their room playing together, then the youngest, Savannah, started crying. She came to me saying that her sister was being mean and calling her names and hit her. I told Micayla to come into the living room with me and had her tell me what was going on and why she was being ugly to her sister. I do not remember exactly what was said, but I do remember what happened next. While talking to Micayla, she was standing right in front of me. I was holding on to her arm, and she suddenly went limp and started shaking really bad. I had no idea what was going on, and I had never seen anything like this. To be completely honest, I thought she was being silly and trying to get out of getting into trouble for being mean to her little sister. This lasted for about thirty seconds, then she got back up. I had her apologize and hug her sister, and they went back to playing.

Several days had passed, and I had not given any thought to what had happened with the shaking and going limp. Then it happened again. I was in the living room floor playing with my daughters, who are now four and five years old, and we were being silly. I started tickling Micayla on her tummy, and again, her body went limp, and she started shaking like I had never seen before. At this point, I was getting concerned because I had no clue what was happening. My best friend looked at me and said it looked like she was having a seizure. I had heard of seizures before but did not know what exactly they were much less what they looked like. I scheduled an appointment with her pediatrician, who basically shrugged it off and could not provide any explanation. The next event changed my way of thinking and started my "mom fight" to find answers of what was going on with my daughter.

It was time to get cleaned up and ready for bed. Savannah had just had her bath and gotten her pajamas on and was lying in bed watching some cartoons until Micayla had her bath. I had just finished washing her hair when I turned around to get a towel from the cabinet. I, all of a sudden, heard splashing around that did not sound like normal splashing when she would be playing. I quickly turned around to see her under the water convulsing again, so I frantically pulled her up and out of the water and laid her on the floor and covered her with a towel. After a little over a minute, the convulsing stopped, and she was fine again. The next day, we went back to the pediatrician, and he said that it sounds like she is having seizures, but without seeing what was happening, there wasn't anything that he could do. For a couple more weeks, she was having these seizures often, and each one would last over a minute. If you do not know anything about seizures, you would not think that a minute is very long, but in fact, you learn fast how long a minute really is. We all started observing her more and noticed that a few seconds before she would have a seizure, she would grab her right elbow, then the seizure would start. Upon telling the pediatrician of this, he referred us to an orthopedic doctor to see if something was going on in her arm that would be interfering with nerves. She and I were sitting in the orthopedic doctor's treatment room, and she was sitting in my lap, the doctor was sitting on his rolling stool looking at her right arm. She grabbed her arm, let out a scream, and went into a seizure. He immediately rolled back, put his hands up in the air, and said, "I can't touch this. This is a seizure, so she needs to see a neurologist." Finally after several months, a doctor finally witnessed what was happening and told me what it was.

We were able to get a referral to a children's hospital in Dallas, but it was some time away. By then, she was having seizures exactly every two hours, and each one was lasting approximately one and half minutes. After being instructed that we just needed to drive to Dallas and go through the emergency room and she would instantly become a patient and we would not have to wait for the referral to go through, my mother and I took off to Dallas with Micayla and went through the emergency room. The nurses witnessed Micayla having several seizures consistently, now lasting over two minutes each. They quickly got her back to do EEGs, MRIs, CTs, blood work, etc. Within three hours, she was diagnosed with epilepsy, and they started her antiseizure medication. The neurologist wanted her to stay the night in the hospital for observation, so we did. They had given her some Ativan through an IV to stop the seizures, and we learned rather fast that this was something else that her little body could not tolerate. She had hallucinations due to this medication for well over a week. We did not think this was ever going to wear off.

Now there is a diagnosis of epilepsy. What now? Again, those two words have a deep meaning, and I promise you that meaning will come to light soon. I was overwhelming myself with information on epilepsy—what causes it, how to treat it, how to respond to it. It is a lot of information but really no answers. We would go to Dallas for her appointments with the neurologists every six months. She would be admitted into the epilepsy monitoring unit for several days at a time so that they could get a seizure on camera while hooked up to an EEG to determine where the seizures are coming from. No luck, still no answers, nothing. It is a very frustrating brain disorder, but we never gave up hope. Sometimes we all felt as if we were fighting a never-ending battle, but we continued to fight for answers.

The school had been notified of her diagnosis, and the school nurses were always on standby. One afternoon, both of the girls were at after-school care, and I received a call that no parent ever wants to receive. I answered the phone, and it was a young man saying that Micayla had multiple seizures and they had not stopped. In the background, I hear the head teacher saying to call 911 because she wasn't breathing. I took off running to the car, left work, and drove like a speed demon to get to the school. When I got to the school, I do not even remember parking, putting the car in park, or even turning the engine off. I just remember seeing the ambulance on the sidewalk, and I jumped out of the car and ran as fast as I could to get inside the school gym. She was lying on the floor with jackets all around her because the after-school teachers and kids were surrounding her with soft jackets to protect her from hurting herself. Two paramedics were standing over her and monitoring her breathing and heartbeats. Her sister is standing over her crying, and I took her in my arms consoling her. Micayla was loaded up in the ambulance, and the paramedics would not allow Savannah to come with us, so I had to leave her there with the teachers and students until my best friend could get there to pick her up.

We are now at the local hospital. All the family has shown up worried. The doctor came in and proceeded to tell me that she was faking it and she was just having behavioral problems. Oh, how this did not suit over me. Micayla was a child that was friends with everyone. She very seldom got into trouble at home and never got into trouble at school. This was not something that she could or would fake. The issue was that the local hospital did not know how to handle seizures and epilepsy, especially with children. Was it their fault? That is hard to say because epilepsy is so unknown. When I say unknown, although it is the most common neurological disease around the globe, its cause most of the time is unknown, and there is no cure, and sadly, the local hospitals really just dismiss the patient because they do not know what to do with it.

Let's fast-forward several years. She started going to an annual epilepsy camp, where she met a young man who became her boyfriend. He too had epilepsy but had been seizure free for a few years. We met his parents, who instantly became part of our family. They told me about the neurological team that he saw and had the technology for finding out more information about his seizures and where the lesions were in his brain and how to better treat his epilepsy. His mother contacted the neurologist's assistant, who then contacted me and got Micayla on the schedule to see this neurologist in Houston who specialized in epilepsy. When I say that this was a dream come true, I mean meeting this family was all by the grace of God. He put this very special family in our lives for a reason. This is how He works. We pray and pray, and if we keep our heart and mind open, we will see His work and see His answers to prayers.

Micayla was put through the mill of testing, testing that we had never heard of because there are not many hospitals that are able to do these particular tests. Because of God working through our life, Micayla's life, they found where the seizures were originating. The doctor started with adjusting medication and adding an additional medication, which worked for a couple of years and when she was one day shy of being one year seizure free and then the seizures started again. Upon further testing, it was determined that she was eligible for a brain surgery that consisted of putting rods in her brain and mapping her brain to see if the part where the lesion was could be removed with little or no deficits. This was successful, and she had a partial craniotomy and had a small portion of her brain removed that was causing the seizures.

Two years and no seizures. Everything was great. She was about to be able to get a driver's license and do everything she wanted. During the night of her two-year anniversary, she had one of the worst seizures that she had ever had, and we were back to the drawing board. There were more tests done and more observations in the epilepsy monitoring unit and another brain surgery that consisted of a laser ablation to remove another small portion of the brain. This surgery, unfortunately, did cause some temporary deficits. She had lost all feeling on the right side of her body. I guess that I should not say *unfortunately* because this really brought out the fighter in her. She went through months of physical and occupational therapy learning how to walk again, learning how to write, brush her hair, brush her teeth. She never gave up; although there were times that she felt like giving up, she never did. She was determined to push through all this and become an independent young woman again, and she did. She had become a warrior. She had become my inspiration and a light for all to see.

Chapter 7

Trials

You might be asking where my other daughter, Savannah, was through all the medical trials with her sister. Many parents will understand when I say that it can be difficult having more than one child, especially when one is having medical issues. She was always concerned about her sister, but she was left out a lot because I was gone a lot to doctor's appointments and hospital stays with big sis. I hated leaving her, but she was always in good care. I would always explain to her why I had to be away, and she seemed to understand, but that did not stop hurt feelings or feeling left out. This was very difficult for me because I knew that I needed to take care of her too. She was so good at taking care of her big sis during the night when she would have seizures, and she knew that it was a big deal, but as a child, you want and need attention as well.

She is exceptionally smart and did so well in school; however, I started seeing her slip into regression and a slight depression. Her grades were slipping in school. She started having difficulties with friends, and I was in a new territory I didn't really know how to respond to. After getting into trouble often at school, her teachers and school counselor had suggested to me to have her tested for ADHD. I spoke to her pediatrician about it, and after the school officials and teachers and myself filled about questionnaires, she was diagnosed with ADHD and put on medication after medication.

Honestly, I never believed she had ADHD, but I never questioned the doctor. Her difficulties in school caused a lot of bullying to her and from her. It resulted in me pulling her out of school and putting her in a home/online school program for the remainder of her high school, which was the best thing for her.

She recently was changed from ADHD and taken off those medications and after testing, was diagnosed with Hashimoto's disease, which she is now being treated for, and everyone around her has noticed a huge difference in her. She had lost her drive and care for so much. She went through some time where she would be cutting herself and talk of ending her life. She now has goals and has been accepted into cosmetology school, which she starts in the fall, and I couldn't be prouder of her. She is trying so hard to find the better version of herself, and she is finding happiness with herself. It has taken a lot to get her there, and it has taken God's mercy to save her from herself.

This world is a crazy world, and the devil seeks those that are weak. No matter how hard and how much I prayed for her, the devil still has a hold on her, but a mother's love and God's love does not quit. I refuse to give up on her heart, on my daughter. She is my curly-haired ballerina girl, and she has so much potential and life in her, and I refuse to let the devil have her. Before I pulled her out of school, a rather large incident happened after school that was detrimental to her and caused a lot a heartache and depression to set in with her. We started seeing a counselor so that she could open up to what happened and find a way for her to stop hurting herself. It took a long time, a lot of tears, prayers, and counseling, but she eventually stopped hurting herself and stopped wanting life to end.

Her journey is not over and is really just beginning. After losing so much confidence in herself, she has been able to pick herself back up, and as Dory from *Finding Nemo* says, "Just keep swimming." She is still having trouble believing in God, and my prayers for her strengthen, and I will never stop praying for her heart to find the Lord. He is with her always just as He is with you, and I have seen Him work miracles, and I know that she will stop fighting Him one day. I believe she struggles with this because in her short twenty years of life, she has seen so much and has dealt with so much hatred, sickness, heartaches, and meanness in the world. Not just for her but for everyone in this world, we have to stand up and keep fighting for good and keep God in this world. As Christians, we need to stand up for Him just as He fights for us. He never leaves us, so why do we leave Him? It is us that gives up and leaves Him behind.

One day, she will find Him, and she will realize how much He has blessed her with. It wasn't the counselors that got her to stop hurting herself. Yes, they helped and gave her options and helped her cope, but it was through Him that she stopped; she just has to realize that. Now when she looks at her scars, she is reminded of that time in her life and how far she has come, and she knows that she still has a ways to go. Sometimes, we just have to change the way that we look at things. Turn something bad into good. Her scars can not only be used as a reminder to her but can also be used to comfort others and be a lighthouse for others to find their way back to where they need to be. Everyone has been through trials and errors, but you have to be able to pick yourself up. This is often easier said than done, and it typically does not happen overnight. Be patient with yourself and be patient with those that are trying their best to help you. Be open to suggestions. Be open to the word of God and let others in. Be honest with yourself, love yourself, and just keep swimming. You have a place in this world, and this world needs you.

Chapter 8

Surgery Time

Her seizures had returned, and she was having them quite often. She was unable to drive herself to work as much as usual because she was worried about having an episode while driving. Either myself, her sister, or grandmother would take her to and from work on many occasions. She always knew when it was not safe for her to be driving, which we were all very grateful for. There was so much that she wanted to do, but she had to wait until someone was with her to keep a close eye on her, such as swimming. She loved being in the pool, and she did not like having to wait for someone to be with her; however, she knew it was necessary. This young lady always took the bad and turned it into good, and she tried her best to keep a good attitude about it. Granted, there were moments where she would get angry with this brain disorder, but she also knew that God had chosen her for a reason.

What was this reason? This beautiful redhead was one of strength and honor. She was full of life, friends with all, and she had a heart of gold. Her friends loved her dearly, and she developed the nickname of "Spitfire" because she would show her fierce side on occasion. She was quick to defend herself and her family, and others knew that she was a loyal friend and coworker. Despite everything she had gone through medically, she never stopped living, never stopped dreaming, and never stopped looking for her true love to spend her life with. She advocated for epilepsy awareness, and she taught others that although you have hard times and things may not go your way, you make the best out of it and turn it into good. All things can be made beautiful; sometimes the most imperfections make it perfect. Negativity can be turned to positivity, anger to happiness if we only open our hearts and minds. That was something that I tried to teach my children, and she got it. God chose her because of her strength, her ability to witness, her love for others, her admiration. He knew that she would be one to brighten the days of others, and she sure brightened my days.

She was no longer a candidate for any more brain surgeries consisting of brain resections due to the location; however, she still had options to become seizure free. VNS implant, which is vagus nerve stimulation, is a device that is inserted and connected to the vagus nerve that is in your neck that sends electronic pulses to the brain to stimulate the areas that send seizure activity and usually stop the seizure. It, in a way, acts like a pacemaker for the brain. She wanted to have this device implanted several years ago; however, we chose the brain surgery route hoping that it would be a more permanent solution. The brain is tricky and smart, and there is so much unknown about it. When a portion of the brain is removed, it finds a way to reroute itself and cannot really be trained on how to reroute its signals. It does what it wants to do, which is why her seizures kept coming back. We were now looking into the VNS implant as our last resort, and if this didn't work, she would continue on medications and continue taking it one day at a time.

This bright young lady was on a path to finding her Prince Charming. She started talking to a young man, and they talked for a while, then for some reason, she stopped talking to him. Several months went by, and they started talking again. I was never one for meeting people online because you never know who it is that you are talking to. Knowing that I was not crazy about it, she did not tell me how she met him until she knew that I had figured it out. He was driving from the Dallas area to take her out for a date, and she had asked me to come over to the apartment that she and her sister lived in so that I could help her pick out the perfect outfit. When I arrived at their apartment, she had some clothes laid out on her bed, and her sister and I were giving our opinions—she didn't take any of them. She said that they were going to the Rose Garden, then maybe to a movie, and it was after that night that she knew she found the love of her life. This young man stole the heart of my twenty-year-old daughter, and I had never seen her so happy. Her family and her coworkers knew everything there was to know about this young man because he was all she talked about and could not wait until he was off work so that he could drive down to spend time with her.

It is time for me to meet this man that she was so goo-goo for. We chose a weekend that he would be in town, and we went to dinner along with her grandparents. I know that she was nervous, and I am sure he was too. I wanted him to be nervous because I wanted him to know that I will protect my daughters at all costs. By the end of the dinner, we all fell in love with him. He was the perfect guy for her, and I knew that he would be in our family to the long haul. This was a blessing, and I loved seeing her with this big smile on her face. She was so extremely happy. Micayla loved her birthday. She loved celebrating and wanted a big deal made out of it each year, but this year was different. She decided that she did not want to celebrate her birthday but instead throw a late birthday party for her boyfriend. I just remember thinking, "Wow, who is this? She never lets us forget her birthday, and this is her twenty-first birthday!" I was quite impressed. She planned the whole party, invited others, made his favorite food, tiny sandwiches, and attempted to make his favorite cake, which did not work out well, I might say. At least she tried, and I am sure that it meant the world to him and he will never forget it.

The neurosurgeon's office called, and she had been approved for the VNS implant surgery. She was so excited, to say the least, because she just knew that it was going to work and she would finally be seizure free. She had the support of everyone, and we were ready to continue walking this journey with her. Her surgery was scheduled for three months away. In the meantime, she and Brandon were having the time of their life. There was talk about getting married. She had chosen the wedding gown that she wanted, and it was absolutely stunning. The dress was long white satin with a sheer lace around the bottom and the trail of the dress. The bodice was a strapless royal blue and at the waist, and halfway down the dress were beautiful silver and royal blue flowers in jewels. The dress was so beautiful, and she could not wait for the bridal show that we were attending in six months, hoping to find a dressmaker that could make this gown for her for her wedding day. She started sending me pictures of flowers, wedding cakes, and wedding venues, and she had called a few places to get pricing. I was wondering if she has talked to Brandon about this and what he thought. She told me that all he had to do was show up. She sent me a picture of the ring she wanted and asked me to send it to him, so I did. He already had plans for a ring though.

December 2, 2022, was upon us. It was surgery day, and she was having the implant put in today. We were at the hospital around five thirty in the morning, and surgery was scheduled for nine. Brandon and my mom and stepfather were in the waiting area, and I went back to prep with her and wait for the surgery team to come in and talk to us. The anesthesiologist came in, the nurse came in, and they gave her the "happy juice" in her IV and wheeled her back to surgery. I kissed her on her forehead and told her I would see her after surgery. The surgery was supposed to last a couple of hours, and I was getting updates throughout the surgery that everything was okay. I received a call that she was out of surgery and in recovery, and they would come get us when she woke up from anesthesia. A couple of hours passed, and I had yet to receive a call that she had woken up yet, so I started getting worried. I went to the nurse's station and asked for an update. I was informed that they were still waiting for her to wake up. Another hour or so went by, and the nurse finally came out and said that she was awake, so her fiancé, Brandon, went back to her as they would only allow one person back there. My mother, stepfather, and myself continued waiting in the waiting room for them to come out. I was anxious to see my baby girl. Finally I saw him wheeling her out in her wheelchair, and we gathered our things and walked over there to them, and we headed downstairs to travel the four-hour ride home.

We settled in inside the truck and headed down the interstate. Brandon had fallen asleep in Micayla's lap, and she was trying to sleep but never truly fell asleep because she hurt. A little way down the road, she was complaining of her stomach hurting and that she was hungry. I'm sure she was because she had not eaten since the night before. We found a place to stop and eat, and she ate a little bit of chicken strips and french fries, although she couldn't eat much. About an hour later, it was time to stop for a potty break, and while we stopped, they both bought some ice cream which was going to feel good on her throat because her throat was sore from the breathing tube. She ate every bit of that ice cream. She had always been an ice cream fanatic, and we loved to tease her about the way she ate it because she had always eaten ice cream with a fork, which was what she was doing now. She finished her ice cream, and Brandon again fell asleep with his head against the window, and she lay her head on my shoulder and slept the rest of the way home. I drove them to their apartment. We got out of the car and hugged each other, and I told them both that I loved them and I would talk to them tomorrow, and he gently walked her inside as he always did. He was the perfect gentlemen to her, and everyone could see how much he truly loved and adored her.

Little did I know that this was the very last time my baby girl would hug me.

Chapter 9

World Turned Upside Down

It was four days before her surgery, and Micayla and Brandon came over to the house to visit. Micayla told my best friend and I a story about something she experienced a couple of nights ago, and there are only a handful of people that she told this to. She was a God-fearing young lady. She loved the Lord and tried to do right by Him, and she was not ashamed of claiming His name to anyone. I am very proud of this. She was very forthcoming, and she prayed for those that were not seeking Him. At first, she did not know if she wanted to tell us what she experienced because she didn't know how I would take it, but it is a story that I will never forget her telling me.

    She came and sat on the sofa next to me and proceeded to tell me that a couple of nights ago, she was asleep and had a vision unlike anything that she had experienced. She said that it did not scare her, and it was kind of peaceful but a little weird at the same time. The only thing that I do not recall is that whether or not she was having a seizure at this time. In her dream, she stated that it was like she was floating outside of her body and was standing over herself watching herself sleep. There were no words spoken in her sleep/vision, but she was just simply looking at herself sleeping. I honestly did not know what to say about this. My mind started wandering aimlessly, trying to figure out what to say. I have heard of this happening to others, but I never believed it, and I have never read anything in the Bible that would help me to respond to this. I also knew that she would never make anything like this up. I pondered on this for a while as she continued to tell the story. I tried so hard to find some words of wisdom, and I was silently praying for God to send me the right words to say but words were just not coming to me. Afraid to tell me because she thought that I would think she was crazy, she assured us that it was very peaceful. To this day, I still think of this and try to find biblical references to this and have yet to find anything.

It was now Friday evening, December 2, 2022. I sent my girls my nightly text message: "I love you, my angels. Get some sleep," and I waited for them to respond because I had never been able to fall asleep without knowing they were safe and sound. I received a response from both of them at 9:29 p.m., so I lay down in my bed and fell asleep. Fourteen hours after her surgery, I was awakened by my phone ringing. It was around two in the morning. It was Savannah telling me that Micayla had had a really bad seizure. The VNS that was implanted would not be turned on until the following week because the site needed to heal first. Savannah and Brandon both knew what to do, and once she came out of the seizure, Brandon video chatted me so that I could talk to Micayla and know that she was fine. She was half asleep, and she said she was okay. The next four words she said were the last words that I would ever hear from her: "I love you, Mama." Knowing that she was in good hands with her fiancé and her sister, I fell asleep again.

The next call was a call that every parent prays never comes through. My phone rang again just before six in the morning, and it was Savannah, and I heard the tears and stress in her voice. Hearing me try to calm Savannah down, my best friend came out of her bedroom and took the phone while I hurried to get dressed. Micayla had had another seizure, the worst she had ever had. Savannah was on one phone with 911 and on another phone with us. Brandon was doing chest compressions on Micayla, trying to get a heartbeat back.

We were on our way to the apartment, driving as fast and as safe as we could. I was beside myself and just praying the entire way. We came through the gate of the complex, and there was an ambulance, firetruck, and EMS truck. I jumped out of the car and saw my youngest daughter on the stairs sobbing. I leaned over her and kissed her head and ran inside the apartment as my best friend stayed outside with Savannah and attempted to call my mother. As I ran inside, I went into the bedroom and saw Brandon in a chair with his elbows on his knees and his hands folded. I looked to my left and saw Micayla on the floor, with one fireman doing chest compressions, one pumping air into her, and the third waiting to take over. The paramedic was injecting her with epinephrine, then with a defibrillator, shocked her to try to restart her heart. I was on my knees clenching my cross necklace, begging for the Lord not to take her, begging Him to take my life instead of hers because she still had so much life to live and had so many goals. She had just found the man she wanted to marry, so I begged and pleaded to take my life in place of hers.

The paramedic decided that it was time to transport her to the hospital, so we followed the ambulance. The paramedics continued working on her on the way. We entered into the emergency room doors, and the nurse at the desk stated that a nurse would be out to get us very soon. We stood there waiting for what seemed like forever when in fact it was only a couple of minutes. The doors opened, and it was at that moment that I knew I had lost my daughter. It was not a nurse that came out to get us—it was the hospital chaplain. He said that he was going to sit us in the family room and the doctors would come speak to us as soon as they were done working on her. I walked in, and Brandon was sitting there in tears. His mom was on the phone with him, and the chaplain was in and out, checking on us. Family started to arrive, waiting to hear, and I honestly am unable to remember which family members were there at that moment. Then the doctor came in, and I prepared myself as best as I could, though it is not possible to fully prepare even when you already know the outcome. She sat down in the chair to my left facing me, and her words were exactly this: "I understand that Micayla had surgery yesterday to have an implant put in and that she had a seizure this morning and you"—looking at Brandon—"did CPR until the first responders came. I want you to know that you did everything right. The paramedics did everything that they could, and when they arrived here, we continued their efforts, but sadly there was nothing more that could be done and Micayla has died."

I remember her words specifically, and I will never forget them. I sat there in shock, tears rolling down my face. My mother walked in the room while the doctor was still in there and looked at me, and I just shook my head. My mother fell to her knees, asking the doctor if she was sure that there was nothing else that could be done, and she assured us there was not. The doctor walked out of the room, and the room fell completely silent. Everyone was looking at me not knowing what to do or say, when in fact, there was nothing that could be said at this moment. I stood up and walked over and sat by Savannah and just embraced her. The chaplain came back in and asked me if we wanted to see Micayla, and I said yes, so he left the room to tell the nurses to prepare her for viewing. A few minutes passed, and he came back in to lead us to the trauma room, where Micayla's precious body lay. Savannah absolutely did not want to go in, and I would not dare force her to do something she didn't want to do, so my sister-in-law and niece walked outside with her.

I stood over Micayla, stroking her beautiful red hair, family all around her sobbing and in complete disbelief that we were having to say goodbye to this wonderful human being that God blessed our lives with. I could not bear to stay in there anymore, so I kissed her cheek and forehead and told her how much I loved her, and I left the room. I do not remember much after that until it was time to leave. I remember walking down the hall with all of my family in front of me except for my younger brother, who was walking behind me. I remember walking past the room Micayla was in, and I gave her one last glance. My knees got weak, and I felt as if I was about to pass out when I felt my brother's hand on my back to lift me up. From that point forward is a complete and total blur to me as well as the next few days after. My heart has never hurt so much, and I really did not want to be around anyone or talk to anyone, but calls kept coming in. People were showing up at my house, and I couldn't avoid people. By the end of each day when the calls would stop for the night and everyone went home, I was exhausted. I would uncontrollably sob, and I was and am grateful for my best friend, who just let me sob, let me be angry, let me alone. My world has been turned completely upside down, and I did not know where to go from here.

Chapter 10

Preparations

The morning of December 3, 2022, is a morning that I will relive over and over again and most likely will for the rest of my life. I honestly thought that this was the worst day of my life, but that day was yet to come because I still had to plan a funeral then lay my angel to rest. At the funeral home, I was doing as well as I could until we were led into the room where the caskets were. It was at that moment when I really did not think I was going to make it through, then I felt a hand on my shoulder and it was my best friend telling me it was okay and we would go in as soon as I was ready. When I tell you how important it is to have a friend that is there for you through thick and thin, I can't express it enough. We all have friends, but make sure you have that true friend that is there for you no matter what. That evening, my sister-in-law was over at the house, and she and I and my best friend were reminiscing and talking and laughing and just spending some time together. It was night outside, but I am unsure of the time of day. I was ready to turn my phone off for the night because I just couldn't take any more calls or messages, but my phone rang. I did not recognize the number, but I knew that it was after the time that telemarketers usually call, so I answered the phone. It was the transplant donor alliance team.

As I have stated several times, Micayla had a giving heart and wanted to help others, so when she turned sixteen years old and signed up for a Texas identification card, she chose to be an organ donor. She asked me before checking that box if I was okay with that, and I told her that I was very okay with that and I was proud of her for making such a selfless decision. She said that when she died, if her organs could save someone else's life, then she wanted to do that. To some, this is a decision that can't be made. To others, it is a decision that is a downright no, and still to others, it is an easy decision. I am one of the others for whom it was an easy decision, and I chose yes to organ donation. When the Lord chooses to take me home, if my organs are viable and could save the life of another, yes, please take those organs to give someone else life. I am no longer in need of those organs as I will have a brand-new body in heaven. The life of another is worth it as every life is precious. Unfortunately there are people who take life for granted and abuse life, but that doesn't mean their life is not precious. The life is still one created by God, and they are worth prayer and worth their soul to be saved.

This call took about an hour, and they had to ask me if I approved the donation of each organ and tissue. They are not allowed to ask if I approve all; they have to ask each individual organ, tissue, everything. The gentlemen was so caring and patient as we went through every little detail. He asked if I needed a break, but I just wanted to get the call over with, plus there is a small window of opportunity to get these organs due to viability, so I told him that I did not need a break. My best friend and sister-in-law were sitting beside me, comforting me, which was exactly what I needed at that moment.

Finally the call was over. I took some time to process everything that I was asked and everything that I had given permission for. My daughter's body was now on its way to Dallas for organ and tissue harvesting. I had to put that out of my mind, and I had to keep telling myself that it was no longer her body; it was just a shell because she, her spirit, had already left that precious body.

Ten days after she took her last breath, we had a funeral for her. It was such a sweet, heartfelt service. Her favorite song was played, "Temporary Home" by Carrie Underwood, along with three other songs. The pastor gave a wonderful message and spoke of her sweet nature and giving heart. It was beautiful. After the service, my family went up to the casket one last time and said goodbye and that we would see her soon. I kissed her forehead and walked out of the side door to get ready to go to the graveside. Everyone that knew this young lady of mine knew how much she loved rolling her eyes and giggling, and at the graveside, I could actually feel her there rolling her eyes and laughing. Here is why…

We were in the funeral procession headed out to the site, and it is sprinkling rain, and by the time we arrived, it was pouring rain. The rain did not stop her friends, family, and loved ones from coming out though. I was right behind the car carrying her body. We stopped. I got out and got under the pavilion as others were doing the same. It was now thundering, and there was lightning. Her beloved service dog, Ace, was terrified, so my younger daughter sat in the car with him. Everyone was getting soaking wet. Needless to say, this part of the service did not last long. Here is where you can start picturing what happens—and I hope that it brings a smile to your face—and where her giggling and eye rolling would have started.

After the service, everyone was going to my mother and stepfather's home for lunch and fellowship with one another. My best friend, daughter, and I were the first ones there, and there were family members that had been there cooking. I was sitting on the couch for quite a while and was wondering where everyone was. Only a couple of people trickled in, but everyone should have been there by now. Then about forty-five minutes later, people showed up. They were soaking wet, and some were even quite muddy. Then I heard what happened, and I myself couldn't help but laugh. To give room for all the cars to get into the cemetery, some had parked off the road inside to let other cars through. No one thought about the ground being wet, muddy, and soft from the pouring rain. When everyone was trying to leave, several of the cars and trucks were stuck in the mud. I can only imagine how it looked using whatever they could to get all these vehicles out of the mud, and I wish I had been there to see it.

Remember reading earlier that there are two words that would eventually change my way of thinking and turn my anger around? Here goes the question: what now? It has been a couple of months now, and I am going through a whirlwind of emotions. I am sad, I am angry, I am confused, torn, beaten down, completely empty on the inside, and I feel as though I no longer have a heart. Where my heart is feels empty as if my heart had been ripped out. I am not feeling love or happiness; quite frankly, I feel absolutely nothing and many times still do, and I do often check to see if I do actually have a heartbeat. I am constantly asking why. Why her? Why would God take someone so precious, so young and healthy, someone that is so full of life and loves life? Someone that just found love and was ready to marry him, someone who just wanted to do good in this world. Why would He take her and not the murderer, the pedophile, the adulterer, the one who just doesn't want to live anymore? There was no reason to take her. Then I would get angry with God because I just didn't understand. We are all God's children, and our children are given to us on loan from Him. I have always known that, and I have always accepted that, but I was not done with her. A parent is never ready to say goodbye to their children, and they shouldn't have to, but then who are we to question His decisions? They belong to Him. I was still mad at Him though. I did not want to be, but I was, so I continued to keep asking Him why.

I was driving myself to insanity. I was not back at work full time yet. I was terrified of leaving the safety of my home, where I did not have to hide my emotions. I did not want to get out and fake how I felt or what I was going through. I still had to be strong for my younger daughter. I had to be there for her. I had to be there for Micayla's fiancé, and everyone was counting on me being better, but that was much easier said than done. One person asked me why I was not back at work full time yet, the exact words being "it has been two months now, you should be over by it now." Let me tell you, you never get over the loss of a child. This person compared it to losing a parent, and it shouldn't take that long to get over it. I have lost a parent as well, and it was very difficult. I was a daddy's girl, and I was devastated when he passed away. As hard as it is to lose our parents, we expect that we will lose our parents at some point, and I believe in some way, we prepare for that, but there is no way to prepare for losing your child. I wasn't angry at this person, I prayed that he would never have to go through what I am going through. I do not want anyone to understand what I am going through because that would mean that they are hurting just as much.

I knew that it was time to talk to someone. I had joined a few support groups, and to the moment, I have yet to pull myself to attend them. I have talked to a couple other moms that lost their children to epilepsy, and I still have an email sitting in my inbox from a mom that lost her child the same way I lost mine. It has been sitting there for four months, and I keep trying to read it but have not made it past the second sentence. One day I know I will be able to finally read it, but I needed help now. I have the serenity prayer hanging on a wall in my home, and I would look at every day, and the words "To accept the things I cannot change" would get to me every time. How can I accept this? How can I accept something that I do not understand? How can I accept that He took her life so soon? What I did know is that I couldn't accept being angry with God. It was time to go visit with the pastor.

Mom went with me to visit with the pastor. He is such a sweet, gentle, sensitive man of God. He is passionate about our Lord. We sat down in his office and opened with a prayer, and I was already crying because I know that I needed to open up to him and find some sort of healing or at least some way of coping. I proceeded to tell him how angry I was and how I just wanted to feel normal again and that I didn't want to be angry. I wanted to go back to work. I wanted to not be scared of walking out of my front door. I wanted to know the answer to why. He proceeded to tell me that he believed that it was okay to be angry and that God understood my anger. I just needed to keep praying and take things one day at a time, sometimes take it minute by minute. The next thing he said was what changed me. He said that I was asking the wrong question. Asking why would only continue to frustrate me because we would never know the answer. I had to stop asking why and instead ask "What now?" These two words, at that moment, changed my entire way of thinking.

I am no longer asking why she was taken so soon, nor am I asking why she had to have epilepsy and why she didn't get the chance to be married and have children of her own. I am asking Him, What can I do now? What can I do now to keep her name going? What can I do now to help make the world a better place? What can I do now to help my other daughter and to help myself?

> But I rejoiced in the Lord greatly that now at last your care for me has flourished again; though you surely did care, but you lacked opportunity. Not that I speak in regard to need, for I have learned in whatever state I am in, to be content; I know how to be abased and I know how to abound. Everywhere and in all things I have learned both to be full and to be hungry, both to abound and to suffer need. I can do all things through Christ who strengthens me. (Philippians 4:10–13)

I knew that I could do this only if I trusted Him fully. I had to start with going back to work full time, which I have. I still work from home one day occasionally, but I am in the office more now, which is a great help. I do still shed tears, and that is okay. I do not fight back the tears because they are healing. I am trying to become healthier. When I get stuck, I look up and again ask, "God, what now?" and He points me in the right direction. I am doing more for epilepsy awareness, and with the help of a friend, we are trying to start an annual fundraising event called Embracing Hope Together in honor of not only Micayla but all those that are dealing with epilepsy daily and all those that have lost their life due to epilepsy.

We are all on a journey of life. Sometimes the journey is rough and bumpy, and sometimes it is a smooth path. Find a way to make even those rough and bumpy roads into something good. It will not be easy most of the time, but I assure you, turning it into something good will make the ride feel smoother. Love your neighbor. Help those in need. Put the technology down and spend time with your family. Cherish every single moment because you never know when that will be your last moment. Laugh often and live each day to the absolute fullest. Parents, know your children. Teach them to be friends and not bullies. Teach them respect and teach them to love.

Raise them to know Jesus. Be a good example to the world. This world needs you in it. God brought you into this world for a reason, and although we all question that reason at times, accept it and be another light in this world that is full of pride, hatred, jealousy. Let your light shine so bright that it blinds the evil doings. Be a beacon that guides others to Him. Be an advocate and help to make this world a brighter place.

About the Author

Susan Linville Branin, from East Texas, is a mother of two beautiful daughters, one of whom sadly passed away at age 21 at the end of 2022. Susan is a double major in accounting and human resource development, currently working on her master's degree in business management. When she is not working or doing studies in her spare time, she enjoys writing and spending time with her family. She is an advocate of epilepsy and SUDEP awareness. Raising awareness of this neurological disorder is a passion of hers. After the passing of her daughter, she hopes to be a beacon of light and inspiration to others. Susan wants, by using personal experiences, be a comfort to those in need and be an encouragement so that you will never give up.